Copyright © 20

Copyright Notice

The Most Important Conversation You'll Ever Have: A Parent's Guide to Leading Their Child to Christ

Copyright © 2025 Goldfish & Grace LLC. All Rights Reserved.

No part of this publication may be reproduced, distributed, or transmitted in any form or by any means, including photocopying, recording, or other electronic or mechanical methods, without the prior written permission of the publisher, except in the case of brief quotations embodied in critical reviews and certain other noncommercial uses permitted by copyright law.

For permission requests, email author at goldfishandgracellc@gmail.com

Unless otherwise indicated, all Scripture quotations are taken from The Holy Bible, New International Version®, NIV®. Copyright © 1973, 1978, 1984, 2011 by Biblica, Inc.™ Used by permission of Zondervan. All rights reserved worldwide. www.zondervan.com The "NIV" and "New International Version" are trademarks registered in the United States Patent and Trademark Office by Biblica, Inc.™

Published by Goldfish & Grace LLC

For more resources and information, visit: www.goldfishandgrace.com

goldfishandgracellc@gmail.com
ISBN: 9798268512991

Cover design by: Art Painter
Library of Congress Control Number: 2018675309
Printed in the United States of America

CONTENTS

Copyright	
Dedication	1
Introduction	2
Chapter 1: God's Love for Your Child	4
Chapter 2: What Is Sin, and Why Do We Need a Savior?	8
Chapter 3: The Good News of Jesus	12
Chapter 4: What It Means to Be Saved-Understanding the Gift of Grace	16
Chapter 5: How to Know If They're Ready-Discerning with Grace, Not Pressure	20
Chapter 6: Leading Your Child to Christ	24
Chapter 7: Baptism — A Step of Obedience	31
Chapter 8: I'm Saved—Now What?	34
Final Chapter: You're Not Alone	37
A Note of Thanks	40
Bonus Resource List	41
About the Author	42

DEDICATION

This book is lovingly dedicated to the parents who long to see their children walk with Jesus.

To every mom and dad who prays over bedtime pillows, answers big questions in the car, and whispers "Jesus loves you" into little ears—this is for you.

May God use your faithfulness in the small moments to lead your child's heart closer to Him.

And to the next generation—our children—may you always know that you are deeply loved, wonderfully made, and called to follow Jesus with your whole heart.

Psalm 19:14 (NIV):
"May these words of my mouth and this meditation of my heart be pleasing in your sight, Lord, my Rock and my Redeemer."

Deuteronomy 6:5 (NIV):
"Love the Lord your God with all your heart and with all your soul and with all your strength."

INTRODUCTION

As Christian parents, one of the greatest honors—and responsibilities—we have is to lead our children to know and love Jesus. It can feel overwhelming at times. What if I say the wrong thing? What if they don't understand? What if they ask a question I can't answer?

But here's the truth: God chose you to be their parent for a purpose. You don't have to be a Bible expert or a perfect Christian. You just need a willing heart and a desire to disciple your child with love, truth, and grace.

This guide will walk you step-by-step through how to talk to your kids about salvation in a way that's simple, age-appropriate, and grounded in Scripture. Whether your child is full of questions or you're waiting for the right moment, this book will equip you to plant seeds of faith and invite your child into a lifelong relationship with Jesus.

The questions to ask and the faith talk at home prompts you'll find here are just a starting point. Feel free to add your own questions and discover new ways to keep faith conversations alive in your home. God often uses the smallest, everyday moments to shape a child's heart.

Let's begin this Holy work together—one little heart at a time.

Notes

CHAPTER 1: GOD'S LOVE FOR YOUR CHILD

Before we talk to our kids about sin, forgiveness, or salvation, we need to start where God starts—with love.

The Bible tells us that "God is love." (1 John 4:8) Everything He does flows from that love—including His desire for your child to know Him personally and live with Him forever.

As parents, we get to reflect that love in the way we raise, teach, and talk to our children. When we lead our kids to Jesus, we aren't just giving them information—we're introducing them to the One who loves them more than we ever could.

How To Share God's Love With Your Child

You can start simple. Say things like:

"God loves you so much. He made you, He knows you, and He wants to be close to you forever."

"Even before you were born, God had a plan for your life!"

"There is nothing you could ever do to make God stop loving you."

Kids need to know that God's love isn't something they earn—it's a free gift.

Bible Verses To Share (Nirv)

John 3:16 – "For God so loved the world that He gave His one and only

Son. Anyone who believes in him will not die but will have eternal life."

Psalm 139:13–14 – *You created the deepest parts of my being. You put me together inside my mother's body. How you made me is amazing and wonderful. I praise you for that. What you have done is wonderful. I know that very well.*

Romans 5:8 – *"But here is how God has shown his love for us. While we were still sinners, Christ died for us."*

Questions To Ask

This isn't a one-time talk—it's a relationship. Let your child ask questions. Ask them questions too:

"What do you think it means that God loves you?"

"Have you ever felt God's love before?"

"Do you know that you're special to Him?"

Faith Talk At Home

Use simple moments to share God's love:

At bedtime → "God loves you, and I do too."

When they mess up → "God still loves you, even when you make mistakes."

During nature walks → "Isn't it amazing how God made all of this—and He made you, too?"

Parent Encouragement

You don't have to be perfect to show God's love. Your gentle words, patient hugs, and daily presence are already shaping your child's view of Him. Let the foundation of your gospel conversations be this: God loves your child more than you can imagine—and He's invited you to help them discover that.

Notes

CHAPTER 2: WHAT IS SIN, AND WHY DO WE NEED A SAVIOR?

Once your child understands that God loves them deeply, the next step is helping them understand why they need Jesus.

This can be hard to explain—especially when we want our kids to feel safe, seen, and loved. But understanding sin isn't about shame—it's about recognizing our need for a Savior.

Sin is anything we think, say, or do that goes against God's way. It separates us from Him—not because He stops loving us, but because sin breaks the closeness we were meant to have with Him.

How To Explain Sin To A Child

Keep it simple and honest. You might say:

"Sin is when we do things that God says are wrong—like lying, being mean, or disobeying. Everyone sins, even grown-ups. That's why we all need Jesus."

"Sin makes our hearts messy and separates us from God. But the good news is—Jesus came to clean our hearts and bring us back to God."

Let them know this is not just a rule issue—**it's a relationship issue.**

Bible Verses To Share (Niv)

Romans 3:23 —"For all have sinned and fall short of the glory of God."

Help your child see that no one is perfect and we are all in need of a Savior.

Isaiah 59:2 — *"But your iniquities have separated you from your God; your sins have hidden his face from you, so that he will not hear."* **Explain that sin separates us from closeness with God.**

Romans 6:23 —*"For the wages of sin is death, but the gift of God is eternal life in Christ Jesus our Lord."* **Talk about how sin leads to death, but becasue of God's love- Jesus offers life!**

Questions To Ask

"What do you think it means to sin?"

"Have you ever done something that you knew was wrong?"

"How did you feel after doing that?"

"Why do you think God cares about sin?"

"Do you think we can fix our sin by ourselves?"

"Why do you think we need Jesus to help us with sin?"

Main Points To Emphasize

Everyone sins—**but God still loves us.**

Sin separates us from God—**but Jesus brings us back.**

We don't need to hide from God when we sin—**we can run to Him.**

Faith Talk At Home

You can use everyday life moments to connect these truths:

After a mistake, say: "That's why we all need Jesus—He helps us make things right."

When you mess up as a parent, say: "Even I need forgiveness sometimes. I'm so thankful for Jesus and what he did for us."

Parent Encouragement

You don't have to make sin a scary subject. When you talk about it with gentleness and truth, you're helping your child see their need for Jesus—and the beauty of His grace. Sin is the problem—but Jesus is the solution. And your child is never too young to start understanding both.

Notes

CHAPTER 3: THE GOOD NEWS OF JESUS

After understanding sin's separation, your child needs to hear the best part: God made a way back. That's the Gospel—the Good News of Jesus.

God didn't leave us in our sin. He sent His **perfect** Son, Jesus, to take our place. This is the most important truth you'll ever share with your child.

God's Rescue Plan

God knew we couldn't fix our sin but —because He loves us, He sent His only Son, Jesus, to rescue us. Jesus, fully God and man, lived a perfect, sinless life, showing God's love and on the cross—he took our place. Jesus took the punishment for all our sins and three days later — **He rose again!!**

What Makes This "Good News"

Because of Jesus, we don't have to stay separated from God.

We don't have to be stuck in sin, guilt, or fear.

We can be **forgiven.**

We can be **free.**

We can be **close to God forever.**

Bible Verses To Share (Niv)

Romans 5:8 —"But God demonstrates his own love for us in this: While we were still sinners, Christ died for us."

1 Peter 3:18— "For Christ also suffered once for sins, the righteous for the unrighteous, to bring you to God…"

John 14:6—"Jesus answered, 'I am the way and the truth and the life. No one comes to the Father except through me.'"

1 Corinthians 15:3–4—"Christ died for our sins according to the Scriptures, that he was buried, that he was raised on the third day…"

How To Talk To Your Child About What Jesus Did For Us

Use simple, meaningful words to help your child understand:

Jesus took your place— Even though He never did anything wrong, He chose to die for you so you could be forgiven.

He didn't stay in the grave— Jesus came back to life to show that He really is God and that He has power over sin and death.

He makes your heart clean— When you put your trust in Jesus, He makes your heart clean and welcomes you into God's forever family.

Help your child understand both the seriousness of what Jesus did and the incredible hope we have because he died and rose again just as he promised.

Questions To Ask

These aren't just facts to memorize. The Gospel is an invitation to respond. Try asking:

"Do you believe Jesus died for you?"

"What do you think it means that Jesus came back to life?"

"Why do you think Jesus had to die for sin?"

"How does it make you feel knowing Jesus did all of that because He loves you?"

Give your child time to wonder, reflect, and ask questions of their own. The Holy Spirit works in those tender moments.

Faith Talk At Home

Find opportunities to bring up the Gospel naturally:

When your child struggles with guilt → "That's why Jesus came—to forgive us and make our hearts new."

When reading Bible stories → "Did you know this story points to Jesus?"

When looking at a cross → "That's where Jesus showed His love for us."

Parent Encouragement

This moment is holy. You're sharing the story that defines all of life. If your child grasps one truth, let it be this: **Jesus died for me. Jesus rose for me. Jesus loves me.**

Notes

CHAPTER 4: WHAT IT MEANS TO BE SAVED-UNDERSTANDING THE GIFT OF GRACE

After hearing the Good News of Jesus, your child may be wondering: "What do I do now?" That question opens the door to the most beautiful invitation: **salvation.**

Salvation means being rescued from sin and made right with God. It's not about becoming perfect or doing enough good things. It's about trusting Jesus, receiving His grace, and beginning a brand-new life with Him.

Salvation isn't something we can earn—it's a **free gift** that we receive by believing in Jesus.

What Is Salvation?

Your sins are **forgiven.**

Your relationship with God is **restored.**

You are **adopted** into God's family.

You will live with Him **forever.**

Bible Verses To Share (Niv)

Ephesians 2:8–9— "For it is by grace you have been saved, through faith—and this is not from yourselves, it is the gift of God—not by works, so that no one can boast."

Romans 10:9— *"If you declare with your mouth, 'Jesus is Lord,' and believe in your heart that God raised him from the dead, you will be saved."*

Explaining Salvation To Your Child

Try saying something like this to help your child understand what it means to follow Jesus:

"Being saved means you trust Jesus completely and let Him lead your life."

"When you believe in Jesus, He forgives your sins and gives you a brand-new start. You become part of God's forever family."

"You don't have to clean yourself up first—Jesus already took care of everything so you could be close to Him."

Questions To Ask

"Do you believe that Jesus died and came back to life?"

"Do you want to ask Him to forgive your sins?"

"Would you like to tell Jesus that you trust Him and want to follow Him?"

"Do you want to be part of God's forever family?"

These questions open the door for your child to respond in their own words and timing. Salvation is a big decision, but it's best nurtured in small, everyday moments.

Instead Of One "Perfect Talk," Make

It A Pattern Of Conversation:

At bedtime → "Is there anything you want to talk to Jesus about?"

While driving → "Do you ever wonder what it means to follow Jesus?"

After Bible stories → "That story reminds me of how Jesus wants to rescue us."

Plant seeds. Ask questions. Be available. The Holy Spirit is always working—sometimes quietly, sometimes suddenly—and your gentle guidance is preparing the soil of your child's heart. This is a time to ask heart questions—not to pressure, but to guide.

Parent Encouragement

It's easy to wonder, "Are they ready?" or "What if I mess this up?" But remember: salvation doesn't depend on you having the perfect words—it depends on the saving grace of Jesus and the work of the Holy Spirit.

Your role is to disciple, not to pressure. Your faithfulness in pointing to Jesus, even in simple conversations, makes an **eternal impact.**

Keep trusting that God is working behind the scenes in your child's heart. And when the time comes for them to respond—you'll be ready.

Notes

CHAPTER 5: HOW TO KNOW IF THEY'RE READY-DISCERNING WITH GRACE, NOT PRESSURE

One of the most common questions parents ask is, "How do I know if my child is really ready to accept Jesus?"

It's a beautiful and sacred question—and one that deserves careful thought and prayer.

The truth is: God meets kids where they are. There's no "perfect age" or checklist, but there are signs of spiritual readiness you can watch for. It's not about whether they have all the answers—it's about whether they have a heart that's open to Jesus.

What To Look For

Here are some signs that your child may be ready to take the next step of faith:

- They are asking these type questions-"How do I go to heaven?" or "Why did Jesus die for me?"
- They express sorrow over sin. Not just guilt, but a sense of wanting to make things right with God.
- They recognize who Jesus is.
- They understand that Jesus is God's Son who died and rose again.
- They show faith.
- They believe Jesus is real and that He loves them personally.

- They want a relationship with Jesus.
- They say things like "I want to follow Jesus" or "I want Him in my heart."
- They can explain the importance of salvation and how to receive God's gift. In their own words, they can describe why they want to be saved and what it means to trust Jesus as Savior and Lord—**not with perfect theology, but with real understanding.**

Questions To Ask

Use simple, open-ended questions to help you understand their heart and see if they are ready. Here are some examples.

First Question -"Why do you think Jesus came to earth?"

Second Question - "What does it mean to trust Jesus?"

Third Question - "Do you want to follow Him with your life?"

Fourth Question - "Why do you think we need to be forgiven?"

It's very important to remember that these aren't tests—they're invitations. You're listening for sincerity, not perfection.

What If They're Not Ready?

That's okay. Don't rush it. Don't fear it. Salvation is never about pressure—it's about God's perfect timing and His relentless grace. If your child isn't ready to respond, it doesn't mean you've failed. It doesn't mean they don't care. It simply means that God is still working—often quietly, deep beneath the surface.

We sometimes forget: salvation isn't the result of the perfect talk or the right prayer. It's the result of the Holy Spirit stirring a heart toward Jesus. And that kind of work isn't always visible right away. Keep nurturing their heart. Keep pointing to Christ in everyday conversations, moments of discipline, and celebrations of joy. Keep telling the story. Keep listening well. And above all—keep trusting grace.

Bible Verse To Share (Niv)

Ephesians 2:8–9— "For it is by grace you have been saved, through faith—and this is not from yourselves, it is the gift of God—not by works, so that no one can boast."

This means salvation isn't something your child earns by knowing the right answers, behaving better, or being older. And it's not something you achieve as a parent either. You don't have to manufacture a moment of decision. You are planting seeds—God causes the growth. God loves your child more than you do. He is drawing their heart, step by step, with kindness and truth and if He is patient— you can be,too.

So if your child isn't ready yet, don't worry. You are not behind. You are not failing. You are faithfully walking beside your child on a path that leads to Jesus and when the moment comes—they will be ready and so will you.

Parent Encouragement

Don't worry about "missing the moment." When your child is ready, God will make it clear—sometimes in quiet moments and sometimes in unexpected ones.

Notes

CHAPTER 6: LEADING YOUR CHILD TO CHRIST

If your child has come to understand their need for Jesus—if they've shown signs of true belief, sorrow over sin, and a desire to trust Him—then you have the incredible honor of walking with them into the most important decision they will ever make.

This isn't just about saying a prayer. It's about believing in their heart that Jesus is Lord, trusting Him for forgiveness, and choosing to follow Him for life. This moment isn't complicated—but it is **Holy!**

When The Time Comes For The Conversation:

1. Pause and Pray Together

Begin the conversation with prayer. This helps calm nerves, open hearts, and welcome the Holy Spirit into a holy moment. Invite your child to close their eyes and pray with you.

You might say something like: *"Dear God, Thank You for loving us so much. Thank You for this special moment. Please help us understand Your truth and feel Your presence. Open our hearts to You. Help us hear You clearly and follow You with everything we have. We love You, Jesus. Amen."*

This prayer helps remind your child (and you) that this is more than a conversation—it's a step toward eternity.

2. Review the Gospel

Before leading your child to respond, gently walk through the key truths of the Gospel. This isn't a test—it's a loving conversation to make sure they understand what they're saying "yes" to. You're not looking for perfect theology, but a sincere heart and growing faith.

3. Help Them Speak to Jesus

Once your child has clearly expressed that they believe in Jesus, understand their need for Him, and truly want to follow Him—you can be confident that their heart is ready. This is a holy, unforgettable moment in their faith journey. It's not about having the perfect script or saying all the right words. What matters most is the sincerity in their heart and their desire to speak directly to Jesus.

4. When Your Child Makes the Big Decision

Celebrate this incredible moment—it's more than just a prayer; it's a spiritual birthday! This is the beginning of your child's new life in Christ, and it deserves joyful recognition. Make it special together as a family.

Remember- This journey isn't meant to be stressful or forced. Trust that when your child is truly ready, the Holy Spirit will move in their heart in a way that's clear and powerful. You won't have to guess—you'll both know. Let God lead, and rest in His perfect timing.

Here are some helpful tools to guide you through steps 2–4! You'll find conversation starters to help you review the gospel with your child, simple ways to encourage them to talk to Jesus, and ideas to make their decision to follow Him a meaningful and memorable moment.

Simple Questions To Review The Gospel

Remember, these questions are just starting points. Feel free to ask any other questions that God puts on your heart.

Questions About Sins:

"Do you know what sin is?"

"Why is sin a problem?"

"What happens because of sin?" (→ Romans 6:23: "The wages of sin is death…")

"Can we fix sin on our own?"

Together, these questions guide your child to recognize what sin is and why it matters. Sin isn't just about "being bad"—it's about being separated from God.

Questions About Eternity:

"When we die, where do we go?"

"Do you think everyone goes to heaven?"

"What do we need to do to be with God forever?"

Together, these questions open the door to talk about heaven, hell, and the importance of a personal relationship with Jesus—not just knowing about Him, but knowing Him as Savior.

Questions About Jesus:

"Why do you think God sent Jesus?"

"What did Jesus do for us on the cross?"

"Do you believe Jesus rose again?"

"What does it mean to trust Jesus?"

Together, these questions gently guide your child toward understanding who Jesus is, what He's done, and how they can respond with personal faith.

Questions About God's Gift:

"What is the gift God gives us?" → Eternal life through Jesus.

"How do we receive that gift?" → Through faith and believing in our heart.

"Is it something we earn?" → No, it's a gift of grace.

Together, these questions help a child understand the simplicity and beauty of the Gospel—God offers us eternal life, we receive it by faith, and it's all because of His grace, not our performance.

Heart Questions:

"What do you believe about Jesus?"

"Do you want to ask Him to forgive your sins?"

"What would you like to say to Him right now?"

Together, these questions help move the conversation from head to heart. They invite your child to respond to Jesus personally, with honesty and sincerity. You're not rushing or pressuring—you're helping your child articulate what's happening inside their heart. These questions are an invitation for reflection, not performance. Let the Holy Spirit guide the conversation.

Help Them Speak To Jesus

Encourage them to talk to Him in their own words. Let them know that Jesus already knows their heart and is listening with love. This isn't about performance—it's about a personal step of faith. You might say, "You don't need fancy or long words. Just be honest with Jesus and talk to Him like a friend. He's listening and He loves you so much."

Your child can thank Jesus for dying for our sins, ask for forgiveness, express their belief in Him, and simply say they want to follow Him. After they've prayed, take a moment to affirm how important this decision is. Let them know how proud you are of their step of faith, and remind them that this is a moment they'll never forget—the beginning of a lifelong journey with Jesus.

Sample Prayer For A Child Ready To Accept Jesus

"Dear Jesus, I know that I've sinned and done wrong things. I'm sorry,

and I want to be forgiven. I believe You are God's Son. I believe You died on the cross for my sins and came back to life three days later. I want You to be the Lord of my life. Please come into my heart, forgive my sins, and help me follow You forever. Thank You for loving me and saving me. In Your name I pray, Amen."

When Your Child Makes The Big Decision

Celebrate this incredible moment—it's more than just a prayer; it's a spiritual birthday! This is the beginning of your child's new life in Christ, and it deserves joyful recognition.

1. Make it special together as a family- Mark the date in their Bible or journal so they can always remember the day they chose to follow Jesus.

2. Take a photo to capture the moment, and consider starting a "faith memory book" to track their spiritual journey.

3. Share the good news with your pastor or children's ministry leader so they can celebrate and support your child, too.

4. Pray together as a family, thanking God for His grace, love, and the work He is doing in your child's heart.

Luke 15:10 reminds us, *"There is rejoicing in the presence of the angels of God over one sinner who repents."*

Heaven is celebrating—and your family should too! Let your child feel the joy and importance of this life-changing decision.

Parent Encouragement

You were there. You got to witness the beginning of your child's life in Christ. What a gift! But this moment also comes with a new calling: **discipleship.** Keep guiding. Keep modeling. Keep growing in your own walk with Jesus and invite your child to do the same.

Notes

CHAPTER 7: BAPTISM — A STEP OF OBEDIENCE

Once your child has placed their trust in Jesus, the next step in their faith journey is baptism—a public declaration of an inward change. While baptism itself doesn't save us (only Jesus does), it's a powerful and meaningful way for your child to show others what God has already done in their heart. Through baptism, they are saying, "I belong to Jesus. I've been made new. I want to follow Him with my life."

It's a moment that invites family, friends, and the church community to celebrate, pray for, and support your child as they grow in their faith.

As Romans 6:4 says, *"We were therefore buried with him through baptism into death in order that, just as Christ was raised from the dead through the glory of the Father, we too may live a new life."*

Explaining Baptism To Your Child:

-Baptism doesn't make you a Christian. It's a response to salvation, not the cause of it.

-Baptism is a step of obedience. Jesus Himself was baptized (Matthew 3:13–17), and He told His followers to baptize others (Matthew 28:19–20).

-Baptism is a picture of the Gospel. Going under the water represents dying to sin. Coming up represents new life in Jesus.

-Baptism is public. It's a way to say, "I'm not ashamed of Jesus. I want everyone to know He saved me."

Acts 2:41— *"Those who accepted his message were baptized…"* **You can remind them: Just like Jesus was baptized, we choose to be baptized as a way to follow His example.**

Key Points For Parents

-Baptism is not required for salvation, but it's a step of obedience and joy for those who have trusted in Christ.

-Talk with your pastor or church leader to set up a day for the baptism.

-Let your child invite friends and family—this is a moment worth celebrating!

Notes

CHAPTER 8: I'M SAVED —NOW WHAT?

Salvation is just the beginning. When your child puts their trust in Jesus, they've taken the first—and most important—step of their faith journey. But now what? The goal isn't just to help them say "yes" to Jesus once. It's to help them learn how to walk with Him daily.

As a parent, you are now discipling a brand-new believer. That may feel overwhelming, but God has already given you what you need: His Spirit, His Word, and your everyday life together.

Colossians 2:6— "So then, just as you received Christ Jesus as Lord, continue to live your lives in him."

Help your child understand that salvation is the start of relationship —not just a decision. Explain that we must grow our relationship with Christ. They are now part of God's family. And like any family, relationships grow stronger over time. But how can we do that?

→ **Talking with Him every day through prayer**
Keep it simple. Prayer is just talking to God like you would a close friend. Thank Him, tell Him what's on your heart, and don't forget to listen too. Short prayers throughout your day matter just as much as long ones.

→ **Reading the Bible**
Start small! Pick one verse or a short passage each day. Write it down or highlight it so you can come back to it. The goal isn't to read a ton at one time, but to really think about what God is saying. Digging deeper with a couple of verses is better than reading a ton and forgetting what you read.

→ **Listening to Worship Music**

Turn it on in the car, while you're cooking, or even while you're cleaning. Worship music shifts your focus back to God and fills your heart with truth and joy.

→ **Surrounding yourself with other believers**
Find a church family, join a small group, and find at least one good Christian friend who can encourage you, pray with you, and remind you you're not walking this journey alone.

→ **Sharing the Gospel**
Before Jesus went back to heaven, He gave His followers a special job: *"Go and make disciples of all nations… teaching them to obey everything I have commanded you. And surely I am with you always, to the very end of the age."* (Matthew 28:19–20)

A disciple is someone who follows Jesus and learns from Him. That means sharing the Gospel isn't just for missionaries in faraway places—it's for you, right where you are! When you tell others about Jesus, you're helping them know who He is, what He's done, and how they can follow Him too.

Following Jesus isn't about being perfect—it's about walking with Him each day. Prayer, reading the Bible, worship, being with other believers, and sharing the Gospel are all simple ways to grow closer to Him. Remember, you don't have to do it all at once. Take one step at a time, and trust that Jesus is with you every step of the way—just like He promised.

Notes

FINAL CHAPTER: YOU'RE NOT ALONE

Keep Discipling. Keep Trusting. Keep Going.

You care deeply about your child's salvation and are committed to discipling their heart. This matters more than you know: you are not just raising kids, but raising disciples.

It's not about perfection. Some days will be messy, and your child may drift or doubt. But keep going.

-Keep praying.

-Keep showing up.

-Keep pointing them back to Jesus—again and again.

Your child doesn't need you to be a perfect parent. They need you to be a faithful one. Remember, God is with you in this holy work of parenting. You were chosen for this call to disciple little hearts toward Christ. Here are ways you can help your child grow in faith at home:

Read the Bible together → Start with a child-friendly version or the book John.

Ask questions like → "What did you learn from this passage?"

Pray together daily → Encourage simple, honest prayers like "Thank You for…" or "Help me with…"

Go to church regularly → Help them see they are part of a bigger faith family.

Talk about Jesus in everyday life → In the car, at the table, before bed. Bring God into normal moments.

Need Help Making This Easier?

We created a simple and powerful resource just for parents like you: **The Family Discipleship Guide**—filled with conversation starters, mini-devotionals, practical tools, and weekly challenges.

Final Words Of Encouragement

You are the A-Team. The front line. The first voice. And God is using you—right in the middle of bedtime stories, school drop-offs, and messy kitchen counters—to draw your child's heart closer to His- So keep going.

The conversations you're having now…

The prayers whispered over beds…

The scriptures memorized in the car…

The small, faithful steps…

They're creating roots. **Deep roots.**

> *Galatians 6:9— "Let us not become weary in doing good, for at the proper time we will reap a harvest if we do not give up."*

Notes

A NOTE OF THANKS

Dear Faithful Parent,

Thank you—from the bottom of my heart—for taking the time to read The Most Important Conversation You'll Ever Have- A Parent's Guide to Leading Their Child to Christ.

Whether you're just beginning this journey or walking your child through a life-changing decision, know this: You're doing holy work. Every prayer you whisper. Every question you answer. Every seed you plant. It all matters.

I pray this guide has encouraged you, equipped you, and reminded you that God is with you in every moment—especially the small ones. Your role in your child's spiritual life is irreplaceable. And I'm cheering you on every step of the way!

If you need more tools for the journey, check out our growing collection of faith resources at: Goldfish & Grace- www.goldfishandgrace.com We believe in the power of small moments, planted in faith and watered with grace.

You're not just shaping their childhood—you're shaping their eternity. Keep going, faithful parent. Your work matters more than you know.

With grace and gratitude,

Brittany Banks- Goldfish & Grace

BONUS RESOURCE LIST

From Goldfish & Grace:

Little Moments, Big Faith: A Family Discipleship Guide withweekly devotionals, memory verse cards, faith challenges, and more.

Jesus Goes With You: A Back-to-School Devotional for Kids- A 4-week devotional for helping kids feel God's presence in everyday school life.

Explore all of these at: www.goldfishandgrace.com

Our list of resources is growing! Be sure to visit the website often!

Bibles For Kids:

•NIrV Adventure Bible (Perfect for early readers)

•The Jesus Storybook Bible (Ideal for younger children)

•NIV Kids' Visual Study Bible (Great for curious learners)

Christian Apps For Families:

Bible App for Kids (YouVersion)

Minno Kids (Safe streaming Christian shows)

Seeds Family Worship (Scripture songs + devotionals)

ABOUT THE AUTHOR

Brittany Banks is a mama, ministry leader, and the heart behind Goldfish & Grace—a creative faith-based resource shop for families, churches, and Christian educators.

Her passion is simple: helping parents disciple their kids in everyday moments with truth, grace, and joy. Through digital devotionals, printable tools, and encouraging content, she's on a mission to remind families that you don't have to be perfect to lead your child to Jesus—you just have to be present.

Brittany has seen firsthand how little conversations about big faith can shape a child's heart forever. Whether it's prayer at bedtime or a gospel chat in the carpool line, she believes discipleship is possible—and powerful—right where you are.

When she's not writing or designing resources, Brittany is likely chasing kids, pouring coffee, or cheering on parents like you in the sacred work of raising up the next generation of believers.

Follow along and explore more tools at:
- www.goldfishandgrace.com
- Instagram:@goldfishandgrace
- Facebook: GoldfishandGrace

Made in the USA
Coppell, TX
09 February 2026